Longman Children's
Picture Dictionary

Workbook 2

Greg Cossu

Published by
Longman Asia ELT
2/F Cornwall House
Taikoo Place
979 King's Road
Quarry Bay
Hong Kong

fax: +852 2856 9578
e-mail: aelt@pearsoned.com.hk
www.longman.com

and Associated Companies throughout the world.

First published 2003
Reprinted 2003

Produced by Pearson Education North Asia Limited, Hong Kong
EPC/02

ISBN 962 00 5318 4

Publishing Director: Cynthia Lam
Publishing Manager: Gregg Schroeder
Commissioning Editor: Christienne Blodget
Editor: Ian Purdon
Designer: Junko Funaki
Illustrator: Teddy Wong
Page layout: Fairwin Design Works

A. Find the animals. Circle.

1. apple   (ant)   2. banana   bird

3. fish   flower   4. horse   hat

5. star   snake   6. tiger   tomato

B. Write.

1.

__apple__

2.

_____

3.

_____

4.

_____

5.

_____

6.

_____

C. Write the words in alphabetical order.

apple, cat, _____

_____

A. Answer.

1. 1 + 2 = _____three_____   2. 4 + 6 = _____

3. 11 – 3 = _____   4. one + eleven = _____

5. five + nine = _____   6. ten + three = _____

B. Count. Write.

1. There are _____two_____ ants.

2. There are _____ flowers.

3. There are _____ camels.

4. There are _____ ladybugs.

5. There are _____ monsters.

Colors under the Sea

Color. Answer.

1 = black   2 = brown   3 = gray   4 = green   5 = white   6 = yellow

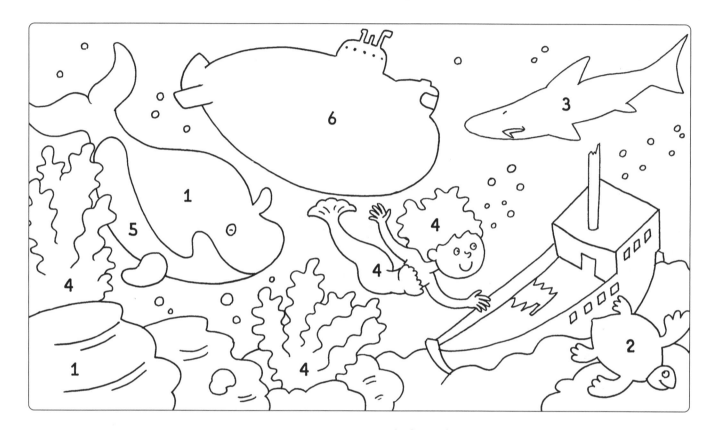

1. What color is the rock?   It's ___black___ .

2. What color is the shark?   It's _____ .

3. What color is the seaweed?   It's _____ .

4. What color is the turtle?   It's _____ .

5. What color is the submarine?   It's _____ .

6. What color is the whale?   It's _____ and _____ .

7. What color is the mermaid?   She's _____ .

Color. Write. Find the words. Circle.

1. a pink

   dolphin

2. a red

3. a purple

4. a pink

5. an orange

6. a blue

7. a red and blue striped

8. a purple and orange spotted

s	j	e	l	l	y	f	i	s	h	r	c	i	s	h	o	r
t	o	p	i	s	e	a	h	o	r	s	e	r	y	n	o	i
e	t	f	u	s	h	o	f	k	l	m	w	k	a	b	l	s
a	y	i	r	o	g	e	o	c	t	o	p	u	s	b	l	c
r	o	s	r	f	i	n	l	s	t	a	r	f	i	s	h	o
l	m	h	k	r	d	d	o	l	p	h	i	n	p	u	i	n

A. Match. Color. Write.

1. It's green.   •   •  _____

2. It's purple.   •   •   _____

3. It's red.   •   •  _cabbage_____

4. It's yellow.   •   •   _____

5. It's orange.   •   •   _____

B. Circle.

1. What's the lettuce doing?   It's (playing music.) / singing.

2. What's the onion doing?   It's dancing. / playing music.

3. What's the potato doing?   It's playing music. / singing.

4. What's the broccoli doing?   It's singing. / playing music.

6 Fruit in the Gym

A. Write.

1. The _____kiwi_____ can do a headstand.

2. The _____ can't do a somersault.

3. The _____ can't do a cartwheel.

4. The _____ can _____.

B. What color? Make three lists.

yellow	orange	red
banana		

Our Busy Town

A. Write.

1. _____supermarket_____   2. _____

3. _____   4. _____

5. _____   6. _____

7. _____   8. _____

B. Unscramble.

1. Where's the museum? | near the It's bakery.

   It's near the bakery.

2. Where's the supermarket? | library. the near It's

   _____

3. Where's the mailbox? | shop. near pet It's the

   _____

Read. Draw a line. Write.

1. You're in the car. Go straight. ↑ Turn left. ↰ Go straight. ↑ Turn right. ↱ Where are you?

    The _____airport_____.

2. You're in the truck. Go straight. ↑ Turn right. ↱ Go straight. ↑ Turn left. ↰ Where are you?

    The _____.

3. You're in the taxi. Go straight. ↑ Turn right. ↱ Go straight. ↑ Turn left. ↰ Where are you?

    The _____.

4. You're on the bus. Go straight. ↑ Turn right. ↱ Go straight. ↑ Turn left. ↰ Where are you?

    The _____.

9 My Family Album

A. Look at the family tree. Write.

8. _____   9. _____

4. _____   5. _____   6. aunt _____   7. _____

1. brother _____   2. _____   3. _____

B. Who's older? Write the words in order.

7   41   60   0   10

baby, brother, _____
_____

A. Unscramble. Number.

1  **2**   **3**  **4**

woesrh   __shower__   ②   leitot   _____ ◯

hutbbat   _____ ◯   benicat   _____ ◯

B. Find 3 differences. Answer.

A    B

1. Where's the comb?   It's in __A__.

2. Where's the soap?   It's in ____.

3. Where's the hairbrush?   It's in ____.

4. Where's the toothpaste?   It's in ____.

5. Where's the toothbrush?   It's in ____.

6. Where's the shampoo?   It's in ____.

Breakfast Time

A. What's different? Circle.

1. toast   eggs   (bowl)   2. cereal   plate   milk

3. glass   pancakes   butter   4. bowl   cup   butter

5. plate   jam   saucer   6. cup   yogurt   saucer

B. Write.

1. Can you read a ?

2. , please.

3. Do you like ?

4. I broke a 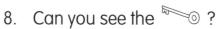 .

5. ? No, thanks.

6. , please.

7. What's the lion eating ?

8. Can you see the ?

9. He's drinking .

10. Do you want some ?

Clean Up the Kitchen

A. Look. Write.

1. It's on the counter.   The ___microwave___.

2. It's on the wall.   The _____.

3. It's on the stove.   The _____.

4. It's on the refrigerator.   The _____.

5. It's on the table.   The _____.

B. Look at the picture. Write *open* or *close*.

1. Did you ___open___ the door?   Yes, I did.

2. Did you ___close___ the microwave?   No, I didn't.

3. Did you _____ the window?   No, I didn't.

4. Did you _____ the refrigerator? No, I didn't.

5. Did you _____ the oven?   Yes, I did.

A. Find the words. Circle.

1.

2.

3.

4.

5.

6.

7.

8.

r	o	n	e	l	e	m	a	r	l	i	x	a	n	e	i	n
s	d	i	f	n	b	n	t	e	l	e	p	h	o	n	e	a
e	c	o	i	p	p	y	k	y	m	k	s	v	n	v	f	g
l	a	r	m	c	h	a	i	r	a	n	k	o	p	r	i	a
c	r	i	o	r	z	n	t	b	g	n	r	l	f	q	r	t
o	p	a	r	v	m	a	g	a	z	i	n	e	n	a	o	e
n	e	d	v	a	c	t	e	l	e	v	i	s	i	o	n	l
m	t	a	v	d	c	o	m	p	u	t	e	r	r	z	x	s

B. Write the words in alphabetical order.

armchair, carpet,

_____

_____

14 Storytime in the Bedroom

A. Read. Color.

1. Color the curtains red.
2. Color the pillow pink.
3. Color the alarm clock gray.
4. Color the lamp yellow.
5. Color the bookcase purple.
6. Color the pajamas orange.
7. Color the slippers blue.
8. Color the quilt red.

B. What goes on a bed? What do you wear? Make two lists.

bed	clothing
blanket	nightgown

16

15 Out in Space

A. Read. Circle.

1. I can see the moon. / (a shooting star.)

2. I can see the sun. / stars.

3. What's that? It's an alien. / the sun.

4. What's that? It's an astronaut. / a comet.

B. Read. Write.

1.  They're in a

    space shuttle.

2.  They're on the

    _____.

3.  They can see a

    _____.

4.  They can see an

    _____!

5.  They're going to

    the _____.

6.  It's going to the

    _____!

A. Read. Write.

1. In the city, there's

   _____thunder_____ and _____lightning_____.

2. At the beach, it's

   _____ and _____.

3. At the park, it's

   _____ and _____.

4. In the mountains, it's

   _____ and _____.

B. Write.

1. What's the weather like?

   It's _____cold_____.

2. What's the weather like?

   It's _____.

3. Is it _____?

   Yes, it is.

4. Is it _____?

   Yes, it is.

17 Spring on the Farm

A. Make two lists.

old	young
cow	calf

B. Unscramble.

1. What's this? | horse. a It's |

It's a horse.

2. What's this? | scarecrow. It's a |

_____

3. Where's the farmer? | farmer The on is tractor. the |

_____

4. Where's the rooster? | is The rooster the barn. on |

_____

5. | ever Have fed you a goat? | Yes, I have.

_____

Unscramble. Number the picture.

1. sifn

fins
_____

2. bursfroad

_____

3. norleks

_____

4. gussaslens

_____

5. candatless

_____

6. smak

_____

7. laip

_____

8. figueldra

_____

9. thabngi tuis

_____

10. loshev

_____

A. Find the animals. Circle.

1. leaves   acorns   (squirrel)

2. nuts   mouse   seeds

3. berries   raccoon   grass

4. deer   tree   nuts

5. acorns   tree   rabbit

B. What do they eat? Write.

1.

The mouse eats

berries
_____.

2.

The squirrel eats

_____.

3.

The deer eats

_____.

4.

The rabbit eats

_____

and the raccoon eats

_____.

A. Write *True* or *False*.

1. The snowman is wearing a hat. _____True_____

2. The snowman is wearing a scarf. _____

3. The snowman is wearing a jacket. _____

4. The snowman is wearing mittens. _____

B. Write.

1.

Let's _____go skiing_____.

OK. I'll get my _____skis_____.

2.

Let's _____.

OK. I'll get my _____.

3.

Let's _____.

OK. I'll get my _____.

4.

Let's _____.

OK. I'll get my _____.

A. Write the months in order.

1.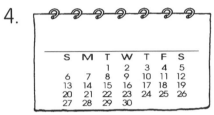
January
S	M	T	W	T	F	S
			1	2	3	4
5	6	7	8	9	10	11
12	13	14	15	16	17	18
19	20	21	22	23	24	25
26	27	28	29	30	31	

2.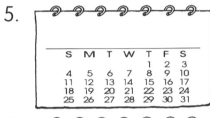
February
S	M	T	W	T	F	S
						1
2	3	4	5	6	7	8
9	10	11	12	13	14	15
16	17	18	19	20	21	22
23	24	25	26	27	28	

3.
S	M	T	W	T	F	S
						1
2	3	4	5	6	7	8
9	10	11	12	13	14	15
16	17	18	19	20	21	22
23	24	25	26	27	28	29
30	31					

4.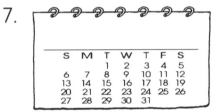
S	M	T	W	T	F	S
		1	2	3	4	5
6	7	8	9	10	11	12
13	14	15	16	17	18	19
20	21	22	23	24	25	26
27	28	29	30			

5.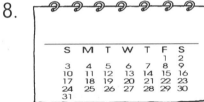
S	M	T	W	T	F	S
				1	2	3
4	5	6	7	8	9	10
11	12	13	14	15	16	17
18	19	20	21	22	23	24
25	26	27	28	29	30	31

6.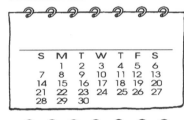
S	M	T	W	T	F	S
	1	2	3	4	5	6
7	8	9	10	11	12	13
14	15	16	17	18	19	20
21	22	23	24	25	26	27
28	29	30				

7.
S	M	T	W	T	F	S
		1	2	3	4	5
6	7	8	9	10	11	12
13	14	15	16	17	18	19
20	21	22	23	24	25	26
27	28	29	30	31		

8.
S	M	T	W	T	F	S
					1	2
3	4	5	6	7	8	9
10	11	12	13	14	15	16
17	18	19	20	21	22	23
24	25	26	27	28	29	30
31						

9.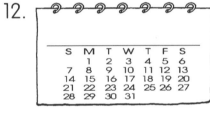
S	M	T	W	T	F	S
	1	2	3	4	5	6
7	8	9	10	11	12	13
14	15	16	17	18	19	20
21	22	23	24	25	26	27
28	29	30				

10.
S	M	T	W	T	F	S
			1	2	3	4
5	6	7	8	9	10	11
12	13	14	15	16	17	18
19	20	21	22	23	24	25
26	27	28	29	30	31	

11.
S	M	T	W	T	F	S
						1
2	3	4	5	6	7	8
9	10	11	12	13	14	15
16	17	18	19	20	21	22
23	24	25	26	27	28	29
30						

12.
S	M	T	W	T	F	S
	1	2	3	4	5	6
7	8	9	10	11	12	13
14	15	16	17	18	19	20
21	22	23	24	25	26	27
28	29	30	31			

B. Answer.

1. Which month is after March? _____ April _____

2. Which month is before December? _____ November _____

3. Which month is before June? _____

4. Which month is after September? _____

5. Which month is before _____? July

6. Which month is after _____? February

22 Every Day

A. Write.

1. **7:00 AM**

morning

2. **6:00 PM**

3. **2:00 PM**

4. **10:00 PM**

B. Read. Write.

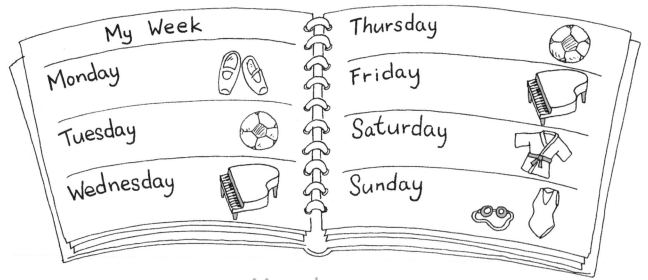

1. I go to ballet class on _Monday_.

2. I go to swimming class on _____.

3. I go to karate class on _____.

4. I go to soccer practice on _____ and _____.

5. I go to piano class on _____ and _____.

24

A. Draw the time.

1.

It's one o'clock.

2.

It's eight o'clock.

3.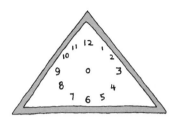

It's six o'clock.

B. Write.

a = ☐   c = ◯   e = △   l = ▭   r = ☆   t = ♡

1. ◯ i ☆ ◯ ▭ △ _____ circle

2. h △ ☐ ☆ ♡ _____

3. s q u ☐ ☆ △ _____

4. s ♡ ☐ ☆ _____

5. ♡ ☆ i ☐ n g ▭ △ _____

6. ☆ △ ◯ ♡ ☐ n g ▭ △ _____

A. Look. Write.

1. ____robot____   2. _____   3. _____

4. _____   5. _____   6. _____

7. _____   8. _____

B. Write.

1. That's my 🚀 .

2. I like your 🪀 ?

3. Where's my 🎮 ?

4. The 🚄 is very long.

5. Put the 🎲 here, please.

6. The 🚗 is my favorite toy.

7. Is this a 📖 ?

8. Can I read your 📘 ?

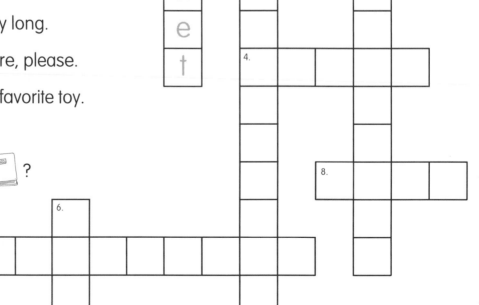

A. Look. Match.

1.

2.

3.

king •

queen •

prince •

• knight •

• princess •

• jester •

• frog

• dragon

• owl

B. Answer.

1. Where's the dragon?

   Near the _____drawbridge_____.

2. Where's the prince?

   In the _____.

3. Where's the owl?

   On the _____.

4. Where's the frog?

   In the _____.

26 Pirate Ship

A. Write.

1. pirate ___flag___

2. treasure _____

3. wooden _____

4. eye _____

B. Read. Write.

1.

Where's the

___treasure___ ?

2.

It's not near the

_____.

3.

It's not on the

_____.

4.

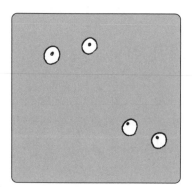

It's not in the

_____.

5.

Where's the

_____?

6.

It's with the pirate

_____!

1 Alphabet

A. Find the animals. Circle.

1. apple   2. banana   (bird)
3. (fish)   4. (horse)   hat
5. star   6. (tiger)   tomato

flower   (snake)

B. Write.

1. apple   2. queen   3. cat
4. rainbow   5. zebra   6. dog

C. Write the words in alphabetical order.

apple, cat, dog, queen, rainbow, zebra

2 Numbers

A. Answer.

1. 1 + 2 = three   2. 4 + 6 = ten
3. 11 − 3 = eight   4. one + eleven = twelve
5. five + nine = fourteen   6. ten + three = thirteen

B. Count. Write.

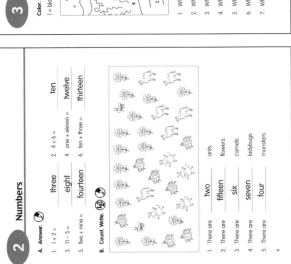

1. There are two ants.
2. There are fifteen flowers.
3. There are six camels.
4. There are seven ladybugs.
5. There are four monsters.

3 Colors under the Sea

Color. Answer.

1 = black   2 = brown   3 = gray   4 = green   5 = white   6 = yellow

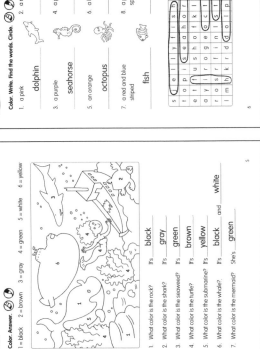

1. What color is the rock?   It's   black
2. What color is the shark?   It's   gray
3. What color is the seaweed?   It's   green
4. What color is the turtle?   It's   brown
5. What color is the submarine?   It's   yellow
6. What color is the whale?   It's   black   and   white
7. What color is the mermaid?   She's   green

4 Colorful Sea Creatures

Color. Write. Find the words. Circle.

1. a pink   dolphin   2. a red   crab
3. a purple   seahorse   4. a pink   jellyfish
5. an orange   octopus   6. a blue   starfish
7. a red and blue striped   fish   8. a purple and orange spotted   shell

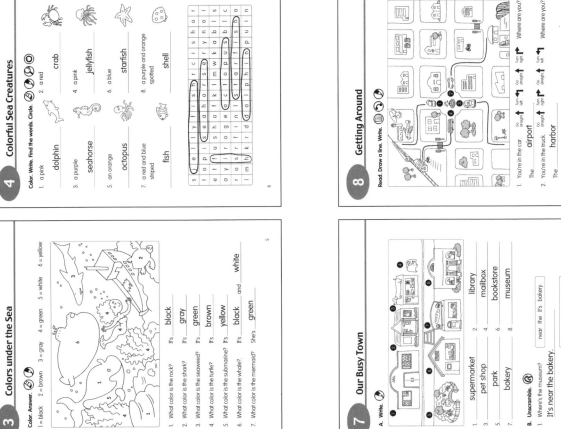

5 Vegetable Party

A. Match. Color. Write.

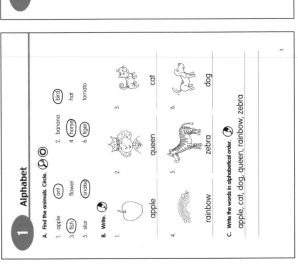

1. It's green.   corn
2. It's purple.   carrot
3. It's red.   cabbage
4. It's yellow.   eggplant
5. It's orange.   tomato

B. Circle.

1. What's the lettuce doing?   It's (playing music / singing.)
2. What's the onion doing?   It's (dancing) / playing music.
3. What's the potato doing?   It's playing music. / (singing.)
4. What's the broccoli doing?   It's singing. / (playing music.)

6 Fruit in the Gym

A. Write.

1. The   kiwi   can do a headstand
2. The   pear   can't do a somersault.
3. The   peach   can't do a cartwheel
4. The   cherry   can   do a handstand

B. What color? Make three lists.

yellow	orange	red
banana	orange	strawberry
lemon	papaya	cherry

7 Our Busy Town

A. Write.

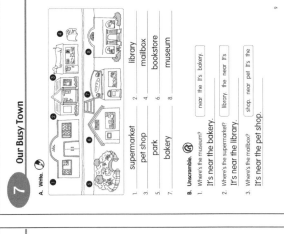

1. supermarket   2. library
3. pet shop   4. mailbox
5. park   6. bookstore
7. bakery   8. museum

B. Unscramble.

1. Where's the museum?   near   the   It's   bakery
   It's near the bakery.
2. Where's the supermarket?   library   the   near   It's
   It's near the library.
3. Where's the mailbox?   shop.   near   pet   It's   the
   It's near the pet shop.

8 Getting Around

Read. Draw a line. Write.

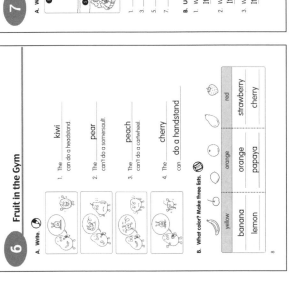

1. You're in the car.   Go straight   turn left   Where are you?
   The   airport
2. You're in the truck.   Go straight   turn right   Where are you?
   The   harbor
3. You're in the taxi.   Go straight   turn left   Where are you?
   The   bus stop
4. You're on the bus.   Go straight   turn left   Where are you?
   The   train station

Workbook 2 Answer Key

12 Clean Up the Kitchen

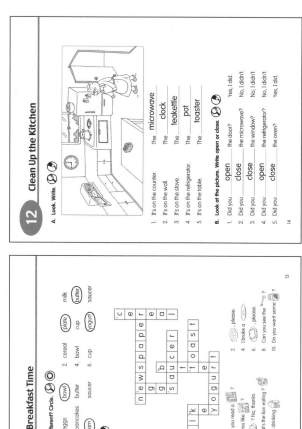

A. Look. Write.
1. It's on the counter. The __microwave__
2. It's on the wall. The __clock__
3. It's on the stove. The __teakettle__
4. It's on the refrigerator. The __pot__
5. It's on the table. The __toaster__

B. Look at the picture. Write open or close.
1. Did you __open__ the door? Yes, I did.
2. Did you __close__ the microwave? No, I didn't.
3. Did you __close__ the window? No, I didn't.
4. Did you __open__ the refrigerator? No, I didn't.
5. Did you __close__ the oven? Yes, I did.

14

11 Breakfast Time

A. What's different? Circle.
1. toast eggs (bowl)
2. cereal (plate) cup
3. (glass) pancakes butter
4. bowl saucer (yogurt)
5. plate (jam) saucer
6. cup

B. Write.
Crossword: newspaper, saucer, toast, yogurt, milk, cereal, plate, cup, bowl, butter, glass

Answers: milk, butter, saucer

1. Can you read a ___?
2. ___, please.
3. Do you like ___?
4. I broke a ___.
5. ___? No, thanks.
6. ___, please.
7. What's the lion eating?
8. Can you see the ___?
9. He's drinking ___.
10. Do you want some ___?

13

16 The Weather

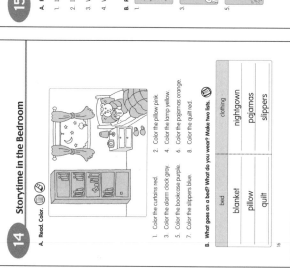

A. Read. Write.
1. In the city, there's __thunder__ and __lightning__
2. At the beach, it's __hot__ and __sunny__
3. At the park, it's __windy__ and __rainy__
4. In the mountains, it's __cold__ and __snowy__

B. Write.
1. What's the weather like? It's __cold__
2. What's the weather like? It's __warm__
3. Is it __hot__? Yes, it is.
4. Is it __cool__? Yes, it is.

18

10 Morning in the Bathroom

A. Unscramble. Number.
woesrh → __shower__ (2)
hubtbat → __bathtub__ (1)
leltot → __toilet__ (4)
benicat → __cabinet__ (3)

B. Find 3 differences. Answer.
1. Where's the comb? It's in A
2. Where's the soap? It's in B
3. Where's the hairbrush? It's in B
4. Where's the toothpaste? It's in A
5. Where's the toothbrush? It's in B
6. Where's the shampoo? It's in A

12

15 Out in Space

A. Read. Circle.
1. I can see the moon. / (a shooting star)
2. I can see the sun. / (stars)
3. What's that? It's an alien. / (the sun)
4. What's that? It's (an astronaut) / a comet.

B. Read. Write.
1. They're in a __space shuttle__
2. They're on the __moon__
3. They can see a __spaceship__
4. They can see an __alien__
5. They're going to the __earth__
6. It's going to the __planet__

17

9 My Family Album

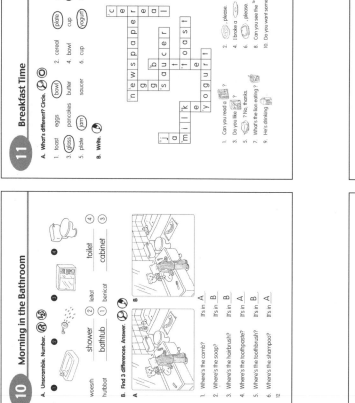

A. Look at the family tree. Write.
4. mom 5. dad 6. aunt 7. uncle 8. ___ 9. grandpa
1. brother 3. cousin
grandma

B. Who's older? Write the words in order.
baby, brother, sister, dad, grandma

7   41   60   0   10

11

14 Storytime in the Bedroom

A. Read. Color.
1. Color the curtains red.
2. Color the pillow pink.
3. Color the alarm clock gray.
4. Color the lamp yellow.
5. Color the bookcase purple.
6. Color the pajamas orange.
7. Color the slippers blue.
8. Color the quilt red.

B. What goes on a bed? What do you wear? Make two lists.

bed	clothing
blanket	nightgown
pillow	pajamas
quilt	slippers

16

13 Evening in the Living Room

A. Find the words. Circle.

Word search puzzle.

B. Write the words in alphabetical order.
armchair, carpet, computer, iron, magazine, sofa, telephone, television

15

17 Spring on the Farm

A. Make two lists.

old	young
cow	calf
sheep	lamb
duck	duckling
hen	chick

B. Unscramble.
1. What's this?
   It's a horse.
2. What's this?
   It's a scarecrow.
3. Where's the farmer?
   The farmer is on the tractor.
4. Where's the rooster?
   The rooster is on the barn.
5. Have you ever fed a goat?
   Yes, I have.

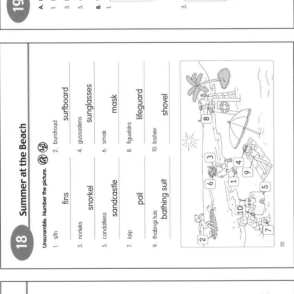

19

18 Summer at the Beach

Unscramble. Number the picture.
1. sifn — fins
2. burstroad — surfboard
3. norleks — snorkel
4. gussaslens — sunglasses
5. condatless — sandcastle
6. smok — mask
7. loip — pail
8. figuerdra — lifeguard
9. thobngl iuls — bathing suit
10. loshev — shovel

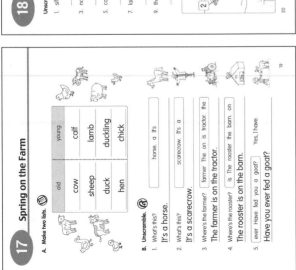

20

19 Fall in the Forest

A. Find the animals. Circle.
1. leaves   acorns   (squirrel)
2. nuts   (deer)   tree
3. berries   (raccoon)   grass
4. (deer)   tree
5. acorns   tree   (rabbit)

B. What do they eat? Write.
1. The mouse eats berries.
2. The squirrel eats acorns.
3. The deer eats leaves.
4. The rabbit eats grass and the raccoon eats nuts.

21

20 Winter in the Park

A. Write True or False.
1. The snowman is wearing a hat. — True
2. The snowman is wearing a scarf. — True
3. The snowman is wearing a jacket. — True
4. The snowman is wearing mittens. — False

B. Write.
1. Let's go skiing.
   OK. I'll get my skis.
2. Let's make a snowman.
   OK. I'll get my mittens.
3. Let's have a snowball fight.
   OK. I'll get my hat.
4. Let's go sledding.
   OK. I'll get my scarf.

22

21 Months and Seasons

A. Write the months in order.
1. January
2. February
3. March
4. April
5. May
6. June
7. July
8. August
9. September
10. October
11. November
12. December

B. Answer.
1. Which month is after March? — April
2. Which month is before December? — November
3. Which month is before June? — May
4. Which month is after September? — October
5. Which month is before August? — July
6. Which month is after January? — February

23

22 Every Day

A. Write.
1. 7:00 AM — morning   2:00 PM — afternoon
2. 6:00 PM — evening   10:00 PM — night

B. Read. Write.

My Week
Monday, Tuesday, Wednesday, Thursday, Friday, Saturday, Sunday

1. I go to ballet class on Monday.
2. I go to swimming class on Sunday.
3. I go to karate class on Saturday.
4. I go to soccer practice on Tuesday and Thursday.
5. I go to piano class on Wednesday and Friday.

24

23 Times and Shapes

A. Draw the time.
1. It's one o'clock.
2. It's eight o'clock.
3. It's six o'clock.

B. Write.

a = □   c = ○   e = △   i =   l = □   r = ☆   l = ○

1. ○ i ☆ — circle
2. h △ — heart
3. s q u □ — square
4. s ☆ — star
5. ☆ i n g □ — triangle
6. ☆ △ ○ ○ n g △ — rectangle

25

24 Toy Box

A. Look. Write.
1. robot
2. monster
3. gorilla
4. doll
5. panda
6. puppet
7. teddy bear
8. action figure

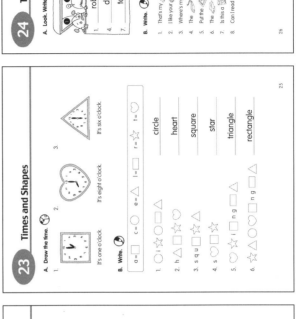

B. Write.
1. That's my ___.
2. I like your ___?
3. Where's my ___?
4. The ___ is very long.
5. Put the ___ here, please.
6. The ___ is my favorite toy.
7. Is this a ___?
8. Can I read your ___?

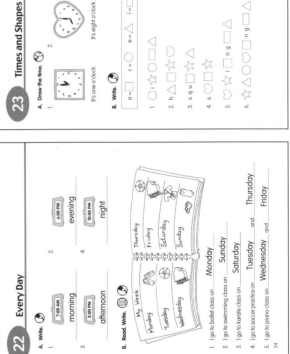

26

Workbook 2 Answer Key

25 Fairytale Castle

A. Look. Match.

king — knight — princess — jester
queen — prince

B. Answer.

1. Where's the dragon?
   Near the **drawbridge**
2. Where's the prince?
   In the **castle**
3. Where's the owl?
   On the **tower**
4. Where's the frog?
   In the **moat**

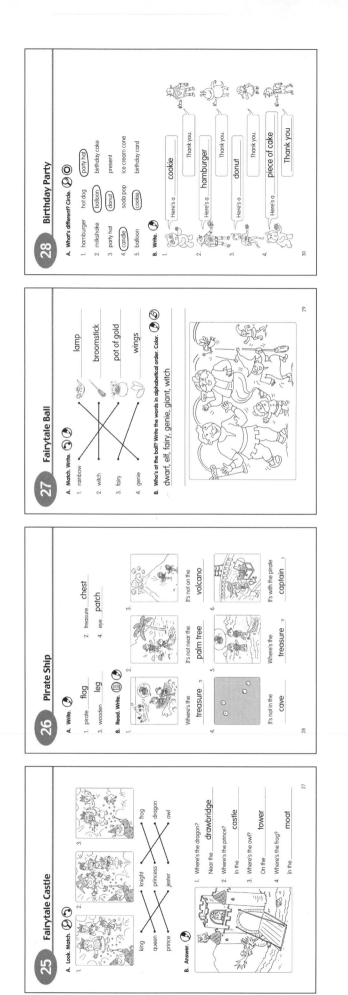

26 Pirate Ship

A. Write.

1. pirate **flag**
2. treasure **chest**
3. wooden **leg**
4. eye **patch**

B. Read. Write.

1. Where's the treasure **?**
   It's not in the **cave**
2. It's not near the **palm tree**
3. It's not on the **volcano**
4.
5. Where's the **treasure ?**
6. It's with the pirate **captain**

27 Fairytale Ball

A. Match. Write.

1. rainbow — **lamp**
2. witch — **broomstick**
3. fairy — **pot of gold**
4. genie — **wings**

B. Who's at the ball? Write the words in alphabetical order. Color.

dwarf, elf, fairy, genie, giant, witch

28 Birthday Party

A. What's different? Circle.

1. hamburger   hot dog   (party hat)
2. milkshake   (balloon)   birthday cake
3. party hat   (donut)   present
4. (candle)   soda pop   ice cream cone
5. balloon   (cookie)   birthday card

B. Write.

1. Here's a **cookie** — Thank you.
2. Here's a **hamburger** — Thank you.
3. Here's a **donut** — Thank you.
4. Here's a — Thank you.
5. Here's a **piece of cake** — Thank you

29 Picnic Lunch

A. Unscramble. Number.

diefr ckichne — **fried chicken** — 5
noydc — **candy** — 3
cpprocon — **popcorn** — 1
esrago — **grapes** — 4
melwataner — **watermelon** — 2
menlo — **melon** — 6

B. Circle. Write.

1. I'm hungry.   Have some **bread**
2. I'm thirsty.   Have some **lemonade**
3. I'm thirsty.   Have some **water**
4. I'm thirsty.   Have some **tea**
5. I'm hungry.   Have some **cheese**

30 Dinner at the Restaurant

A. Answer.

1. A. What would you like?
   B. I'll have **pizza** please.
2. A. What would you like?
   B. I'll have **rice** please.
3. A. What would you like?
   B. I'll have **soup** please.
4. A. What would you like?
   B. I'll have **fish** please.

B. Find the words. Circle.

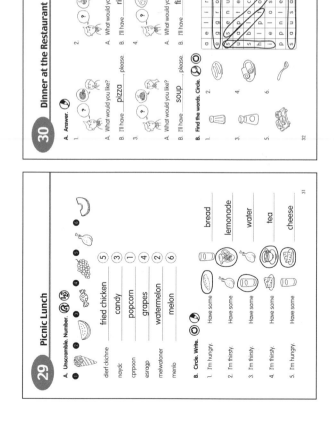

31 Bears Go Camping

A. Read. Write.

1. This bear wants to **go swimming** near the waterfall.
2. This bear wants to **go kayaking** in the lake.
3. This bear wants to **go hiking** in the mountains.
4. This bear wants to **go fishing** in the river.

B. Look at the pictures. Answer.

1. Where's the backpack?   It's in **3**
2. Where's the campfire?   It's in **4**
3. Where's the tent?   It's in **2**
4. Where's the sleeping bag?   It's in **1**

32 Playtime in the Park

A. What do you need? Match.

1. ride a bike — bike
2. play baseball — glove
   knee pads
3. go skating — helmet
   bat
   in-line skates

B. Read. Number. Write.

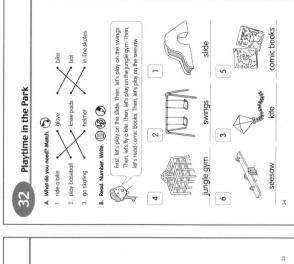

First, let's play on the slide. Then, let's play on the swings. Then, let's fly a kite. Then, let's play on the jungle gym. Then, let's read comic books. Then, let's play on the seesaw.

4 — jungle gym   2 — swings   1 — slide
6 — seesaw   3 — kite   5 — comic books

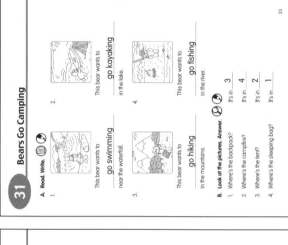

33 African Plains

A. Find the animals. Circle.
1. (hyena) beak trunk
2. tall grass (buffalo) water hole
3. horn acacia tree (hippopotamus)
4. tusk (cheetah) beak
5. (rhinoceros) trunk tusk

B. Draw a line to the water hole. Answer.

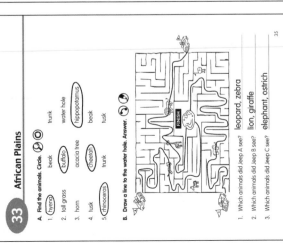

1. Which animals did Jeep A see? leopard, zebra
2. Which animals did Jeep B see? lion, giraffe
3. Which animals did Jeep C see? elephant, ostrich

35

34 Tropical Rainforests

A. Count. Write.

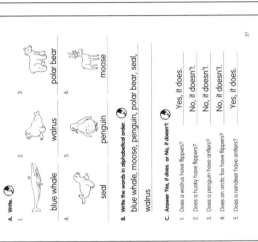

1. There are six   frogs
2. There are eight   snakes
3. There are five   parrots
4. There are two   monkeys

B. Read. Circle.
1. This animal has fangs.
   a. orangutan   b. (jaguar)
2. This animal has feathers.
   a. (toucan)   b. monkey
3. This animal can swim.
   a. (piranha)   b. parrot
4. This animal can climb.
   a. piranha   b. (orangutang)

36

35 Polar Regions

A. Write.

1. blue whale   2. walrus   3. polar bear
4. seal   5. penguin   6. moose

B. Write the words in alphabetical order.
blue whale, moose, penguin, polar bear, seal, walrus

C. Answer Yes, it does. or No, it doesn't.
1. Does a walrus have flippers? Yes, it does.
2. Does a husky have flippers? No, it doesn't.
3. Does a penguin have antlers? No, it doesn't.
4. Does an arctic fox have flippers? No, it doesn't.
5. Does a reindeer have antlers? Yes, it does.

37

36 Australian Outback

Color. Answer.
1 = black   2 = blue   3 = brown   4 = gray   5 = green   6 = red

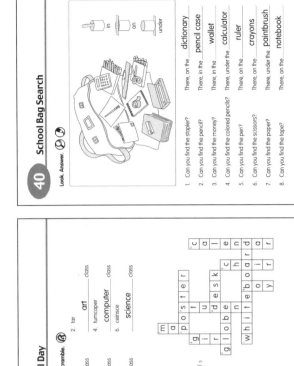

1. Which animal is in the pouch? The joey
2. Which animal is near the rock? The platypus
3. Which animal is near the billabong? The wombat
4. Which animal is in the gum tree? The koala
5. Which animal is in the billabong? The crocodile
6. Which animal is near the didgeridoo? The emu

38

37 Deserts

A. Follow the path. Write.

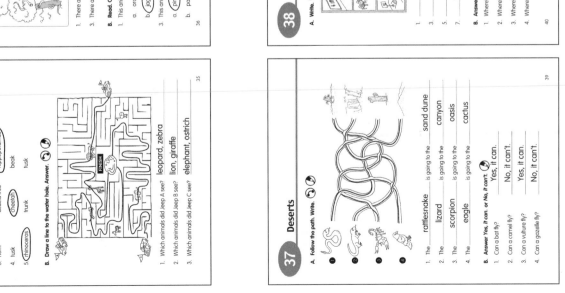

1. The rattlesnake is going to the sand dune
2. The lizard is going to the canyon
3. The scorpion is going to the oasis
4. The eagle is going to the cactus

B. Answer Yes, it can. or No, it can't.
1. Can a bat fly? Yes, it can.
2. Can a camel fly? No, it can't.
3. Can a vulture fly? Yes, it can.
4. Can a gazelle fly? No, it can't.

39

38 The Schoolyard

A. Write.

1. office   2. library
3. classroom   4. restroom
5. gym   6. lunchroom
7. music room

B. Answer.
1. Where's the office? It's next to the library
2. Where's the restroom? It's next to the gym
3. Where's the music room? It's next to the lunchroom
4. Where's the classroom? It's next to the library

40

39 School Day

A. What class is it? Unscramble.
1. glEnish   English class
2. tar   art class
3. surmic   music class
4. turncoper   computer class
5. tornh   math class
6. ceinsce   science class

B. Write.
1. I can see the
2. I like that ___ best.
3. He's a
4. Can you spell ___?
5. Where's Italy on the ___?
6. Go to your
7. Come to the
8. Can you spell ___?
9. Sit on your
10. Look at the

(crossword: map, poster, globe, desk, whiteboard, chair, ruler)

41

40 School Bag Search

Look. Answer.

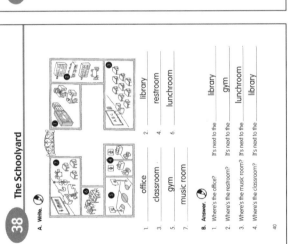
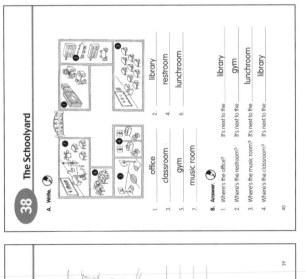

in   on   under

1. Can you find the stapler? There, on the dictionary
2. Can you find the pencil? There, in the pencil case
3. Can you find the money? There, in the wallet
4. Can you find the colored pencils? There, under the calculator
5. Can you find the pen? There, on the ruler
6. Can you find the scissors? There, on the crayons
7. Can you find the paper? There, under the paintbrush
8. Can you find the tape? There, on the notebook

42

44 Bugs and Little Creatures

A. Find the words. Circle.

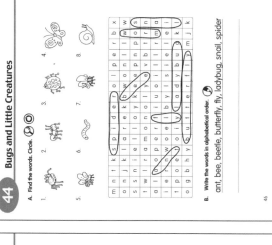

B. Write the words in alphabetical order.

ant, bee, beetle, butterfly, fly, ladybug, snail, spider

46

48 At the Vet's

A. Look at the tiger x-rays. Write.

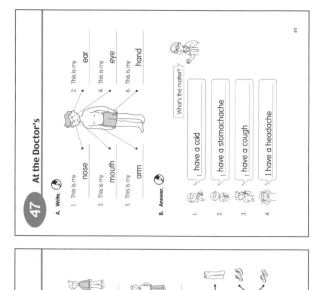

1. tail
2. paw
3. leg
4. back

B. Answer Yes, it does. or No, it doesn't. Write.

1. Does a tiger have hair? No, it doesn't.
2. Does a tiger have whiskers? Yes, it does.
3. Does a tiger have fingers? No, it doesn't.
4. Does a tiger have a tongue? Yes, it does.
5. Does a tiger have teeth? Yes, it does.
6. Does a tiger have bones? Yes, it does.
7. Does a tiger have fur? Yes, it does.
8. Does a tiger have toes? No, it doesn't.

50

43 Pets

A. Write.

1. cat
2. turtle
3. bird
4. rabbit
5. dog
6. goldfish

B. Unscramble. Circle.

1. a rabbit Is fast? — Is a rabbit fast? Yes, it is. / No, it isn't.
2. Is kitten small? a — Is a kitten small? Yes, it is. / No, it isn't.
3. slow? gecko Is a — Is a gecko slow? Yes, it is. / (No, it isn't.)
4. big? goldfish a Is — Is a goldfish big? Yes, it is. / (No, it isn't.)
5. turtle fast? Is a — Is a turtle fast? Yes, it is. / (No, it isn't.)

45

42 Animal Orchestra

A. Unscramble. Number.

deorrecr	recorder	5
tulfe	flute	1
ongbo mdrus	bongo drums	6
ruigat	guitar	2
ilovin	violin	3
petrumt	trumpet	4

B. Which instruments do you and don't you blow? Make two lists.

recorder	guitar
flute	violin
trumpet	bongo drums

44

47 At the Doctor's

A. Write.

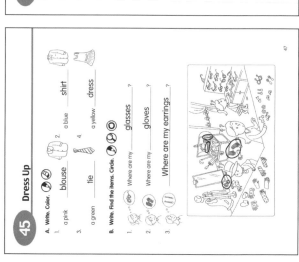

1. This is my nose
2. This is my ear
3. This is my mouth
4. This is my eye
5. This is my arm
6. This is my hand

B. Answer. What's the matter?

1. I have a cold
2. I have a stomachache
3. I have a cough
4. I have a headache

49

46 My Favorite Clothes

A. What's different? Circle. Write.

1. sandals
2. cap
3. belt
4. watch

B. Read. Match.

1. He's wearing a T-shirt, jeans and hiking boots.
2. She's wearing a sweater, a skirt and shoes.
3. She's wearing a raincoat, boots and pants.

48

41 Sports Day

A. Look. Match.

1. She's at the starting line.
2. She comes in first.
3. She's running a race.
4. She's at the finish line.

B. Write the sentences in order.

1. She's at the starting line
2. She's running a race
3. She's at the finish line
4. She comes in first

43

45 Dress Up

A. Write. Color.

1. a pink blouse
2. a blue shirt
3. a green tie
4. a yellow dress

B. Write. Find the items. Circle.

1. Where are my glasses?
2. Where are my gloves?
3. Where are my earrings?

47

49 The Fairground

How do they look? Color the people. Write.

blue = wet   brown = dirty   gold = beautiful   gray = sad
green = short   orange = large   red = tall   yellow = happy

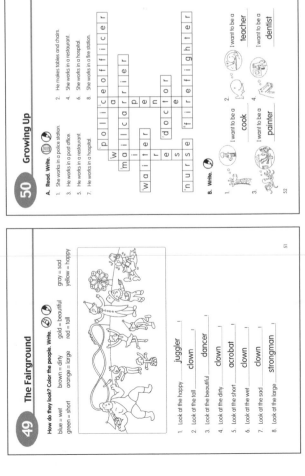

1. Look at the happy   juggler
2. Look at the tall   clown
3. Look at the beautiful   dancer
4. Look at the dirty   clown
5. Look at the short   acrobat
6. Look at the wet   clown
7. Look at the sad   clown
8. Look at the large   strongman

51

50 Growing Up

A. Read. Write.

1. She works in a police station.
2. He makes tables and chairs.
3. He works in a post office.
4. She works in a restaurant.
5. He works in a restaurant.
6. She works in a hospital.
7. He works in a hospital.
8. She works in a fire station.

p o l i c e o f f i c e r
m a i l c a r r i e r
w   i   p
a   e   n
waiter   d o c t o r
r   s   e
nurse   f i r e f i g h t e r

B. Write.

1. I want to be a   cook
2. I want to be a   teacher
3. I want to be a   painter
4. I want to be a   dentist

52

A. Match. Write.

1. rainbow •

2. witch •

3. fairy •

4. genie •

• _____

• _____

• ____ pot of gold ____

• _____

B. Who's at the ball? Write the words in alphabetical order. Color.

dwarf, elf, _____

_____

28   Birthday Party

A. What's different? Circle.

1. hamburger	hot dog	(party hat)
2. milkshake	balloon	birthday cake
3. party hat	donut	present
4. candle	soda pop	ice cream cone
5. balloon	cookie	birthday card

B. Write.

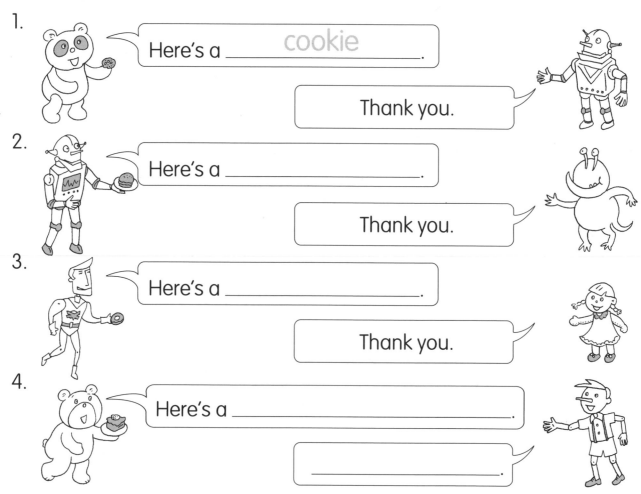

1. Here's a _____cookie_____.
   Thank you.

2. Here's a _____.
   Thank you.

3. Here's a _____.
   Thank you.

4. Here's a _____.
   _____.

A. Unscramble. Number.

 1   2   3   4   5   6

dierf ckichne   _____fried chicken_____   (5)

naydc   _____ ( )

cprpoon   _____ ( )

esragp   _____ ( )

melwatoner   _____ ( )

menlo   _____ ( )

B. Circle. Write.

1. I'm hungry.   Have some   _____bread_____.

2. I'm thirsty.   Have some   _____.

3. I'm thirsty.   Have some   _____.

4. I'm thirsty.   Have some   _____.

5. I'm hungry.   Have some   _____.

31

A. Answer.

1.

A. What would you like?

B. I'll have _____pizza_____, please.

2.

A. What would you like?

B. I'll have _____, please.

3.

A. What would you like?

B. I'll have _____, please.

4.

A. What would you like?

B. I'll have _____, please.

B. Find the words. Circle.

1.

2.

3.

4.

5.

6.

a	e	l	i	r	o	o	n	k
e	g	g	r	o	l	l	s	s
s	s	e	n	u	r	n	e	o
u	a	p	t	e	v	l	o	y
s	b	l	o	c	d	o	p	s
h	l	p	t	o	p	h	f	a
i	e	l	o	s	n	l	s	u
p	p	n	l	e	a	e	e	c
s	a	u	s	a	g	e	s	e

Bears Go Camping

A. Read. Write.

1.

This bear wants to

_____go swimming_____

near the waterfall.

2.

This bear wants to

_____

in the lake.

3.

This bear wants to

_____

in the mountains.

4.

This bear wants to

_____

in the river.

B. Look at the pictures. Answer.

1. Where's the backpack?   It's in ___3___.

2. Where's the campfire?   It's in _____.

3. Where's the tent?   It's in _____.

4. Where's the sleeping bag?   It's in _____.

A. What do you need? Match.

1. ride a bike •   • glove   •   • bike

2. play baseball •   • knee pads •   • bat

3. go skating •   • helmet   •   • in-line skates

B. Read. Number. Write.

First, let's play on the slide. Then, let's play on the swings. Then, let's fly a kite. Then, let's play on the jungle gym. Then, let's read comic books. Then, let's play on the seesaw.

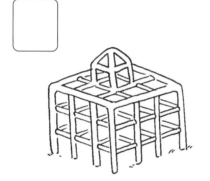

slide

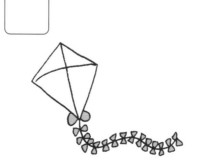

A. Find the animals. Circle.

1. (hyena)   beak   trunk

2. tall grass   buffalo   water hole

3. horn   acacia tree   hippopotamus

4. tusk   cheetah   beak

5. rhinoceros   trunk   tusk

B. Draw a line to the water hole. Answer.

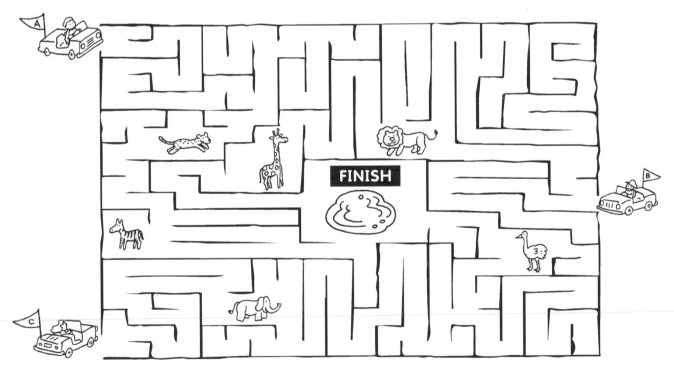

1. Which animals did Jeep A see?   leopard,_____

2. Which animals did Jeep B see?   _____

3. Which animals did Jeep C see?   _____

A. Count. Write.

1. There are six ___*frogs*___.

2. There are eight _____.

3. There are five _____.

4. There are two _____.

B. Read. Circle.

1. This animal has fangs.

   a. orangutang

   b. (jaguar)

2. This animal has feathers.

   a. toucan

   b. monkey

3. This animal can swim.

   a. piranha

   b. parrot

4. This animal can climb.

   a. piranha

   b. orangutang

35 Polar Regions

A. Write.

1.
blue whale

2.
_____

3.
_____

4.
_____

5.
_____

6.
_____

B. Write the words in alphabetical order.

blue whale, moose, _____

_____

C. Answer *Yes, it does.* or *No, it doesn't.*

1. Does a walrus have flippers?   Yes, it does.

2. Does a husky have flippers?   _____

3. Does a penguin have antlers?   _____

4. Does an arctic fox have flippers?   _____

5. Does a reindeer have antlers?   _____

Color. Answer.

1 = black   2 = blue   3 = brown   4 = gray   5 = green   6 = red

1. Which animal is in the pouch?   The _____ joey _____.

2. Which animal is near the rock?   The _____.

3. Which animal is near the billabong?   The _____.

4. Which animal is in the gum tree?   The _____.

5. Which animal is in the billabong?   The _____.

6. Which animal is near the didgeridoo?   The _____.

A. Follow the path. Write.

1. The _____rattlesnake_____ is going to the _____sand dune_____.

2. The _____ is going to the _____.

3. The _____ is going to the _____.

4. The _____ is going to the _____.

B. Answer _Yes, it can._ or _No, it can't._

1. Can a bat fly? _____Yes, it can._____

2. Can a camel fly? _____

3. Can a vulture fly? _____

4. Can a gazelle fly? _____

A. Write.

1. _____office_____

2. _____

3. _____

4. _____

5. _____

6. _____

7. _____

B. Answer.

1. Where's the office?   It's next to the _____library_____.

2. Where's the restroom?   It's next to the _____.

3. Where's the music room?   It's next to the _____.

4. Where's the classroom?   It's next to the _____.

39 **School Day**

A. What class is it? Unscramble.

1. glEnish

   _____English_____ class

2. tar

   _____ class

3. sumic

   _____ class

4. tumcoper

   _____ class

5. tamh

   _____ class

6. ceinsce

   _____ class

B. Write.

1. I can see the [ ] .

2. I like that [ ] best.

3. He's a  .

4. Can you spell [ ] ?

5. Where's Italy on the [ ] ?

6. Go to your .

7. Come to the [ ] .

8. Can you spell [ ] ?

9. Sit on your [ ] .

10. Look at the [ ] .

Look. Answer.

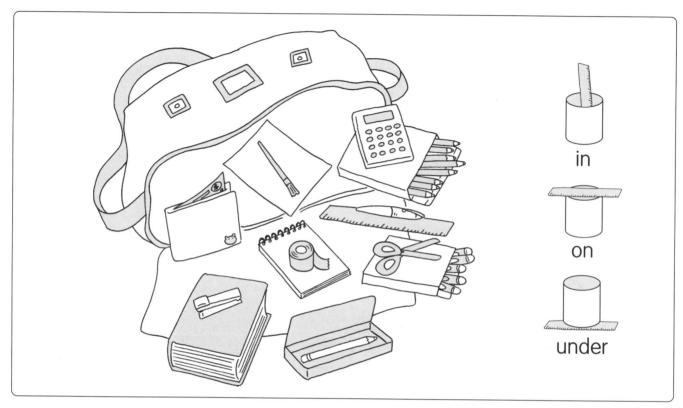

in

on

under

1. Can you find the stapler?   There, on the ___dictionary___.

2. Can you find the pencil?   There, in the _____.

3. Can you find the money?   There, in the _____.

4. Can you find the colored pencils? There, under the _____.

5. Can you find the pen?   There, on the _____.

6. Can you find the scissors?   There, on the _____.

7. Can you find the paper?   There, under the _____.

8. Can you find the tape?   There, on the _____.

A. Look. Match.

1.

•   •   She's at the starting line.

2.

•   •   She comes in first.

3.

•   •   She's running a race.

4.

•   •   She's at the finish line.

B. Write the sentences in order.

1. She's _____ at the starting line _____.

2. She's _____.

3. She's _____.

4. She _____.

Animal Orchestra

A. Unscramble. Number.

①  ② ③ ④ ⑤  ⑥

deorrecr _____recorder_____ ⑤

tulfe _____ ◯

ongbo mdrus _____ ◯

ruigat _____ ◯

iloivn _____ ◯

petrumt _____ ◯

B. Which instruments do you and don't you blow? Make two lists.

recorder	guitar

44

A. Write.

1.

cat

2.

_____

3.

_____

4.

_____

5.

_____

6.

_____

B. Unscramble. Circle.

1. [a   rabbit   Is   fast?]

Is a rabbit fast?
_____   (Yes, it is.) / No, it isn't.

2. [Is   kitten   small?   a]

_____   Yes, it is. / No, it isn't.

3. [slow?   gecko   Is   a]

_____   Yes, it is. / No, it isn't.

4. [Is   big?   goldfish   a]

_____   Yes, it is. / No, it isn't.

5. [turtle   fast?   Is   a]

_____   Yes, it is./No, it isn't.

Bugs and Little Creatures

A. Find the words. Circle.

1.

2.

3.

4.

5.

6.

7.

8.

m	n	t	k	s	p	i	d	e	r	o	l	p	e	r	b	x
o	n	j	k	l	a	r	e	k	b	w	o	n	l	l	w	w
s	s	n	i	e	l	l	o	y	k	e	e	p	n	p	o	s
t	w	l	r	a	m	o	n	o	l	y	e	v	b	t	r	n
a	l	a	o	p	e	r	f	i	u	o	i	l	l	r	m	a
i	e	r	n	w	o	e	l	b	y	l	s	i	e	l	e	i
t	p	o	e	t	o	i	y	l	a	d	y	b	u	g	k	l
o	g	b	h	y	b	u	t	t	e	r	f	l	y	m	j	k

B. Write the words in alphabetical order.

ant, bee,

A. Write. Color.

1.
a pink _____blouse_____

2.
a blue _____

3.
a green _____

4.
a yellow _____

B. Write. Find the items. Circle.

1.  Where are my _____glasses_____?

2. Where are my _____?

3. _____?

My Favorite Clothes

A. What's different? Circle. Write.

1.

__sandals__

2.

3.

4.

B. Read. Match.

1. He's wearing a T-shirt, jeans and hiking boots.

2. She's wearing a sweater, a skirt and shoes.

3. She's wearing a raincoat, boots and pants.

At the Doctor's

A. Write.

1. This is my

_____nose_____ .

2. This is my

_____ .

3. This is my

_____ .

4. This is my

_____ .

5. This is my

_____ .

6. This is my

_____ .

B. Answer.

What's the matter?

1.   I _____have a cold_____ .

2.   I _____ .

3.   I _____ .

4.   _____ .

48 At the Vet's

A. Look at the tiger x-rays. Write.

1.  2. 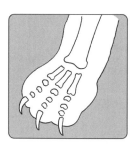 3. 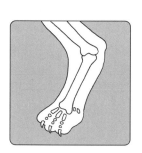 4.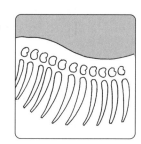

1. _____tail_____   2. _____

3. _____   4. _____

B. Answer *Yes, it does.* or *No, it doesn't.*

1. Does a tiger have hair?   _____No, it doesn't._____

2. Does a tiger have whiskers?   _____

3. Does a tiger have fingers?   _____

4. Does a tiger have a tongue?   _____

5. Does a tiger have teeth?   _____

6. Does a tiger have bones?   _____

7. Does a tiger have fur?   _____

8. Does a tiger have toes?   _____

How do they look? Color the people. Write.

blue = wet   brown = dirty   gold = beautiful   gray = sad
green = short   orange = large   red = tall   yellow = happy

1. Look at the happy ___juggler___ !

2. Look at the tall _____!

3. Look at the beautiful _____!

4. Look at the dirty _____!

5. Look at the short _____!

6. Look at the wet _____!

7. Look at the sad _____!

8. Look at the large _____!

A. Read. Write.

1. She works in a police station.
2. He makes tables and chairs.
3. He works in a post office.
4. She works in a restaurant.
5. He works in a restaurant.
6. She works in a hospital.
7. He works in a hospital.
8. She works in a fire station.

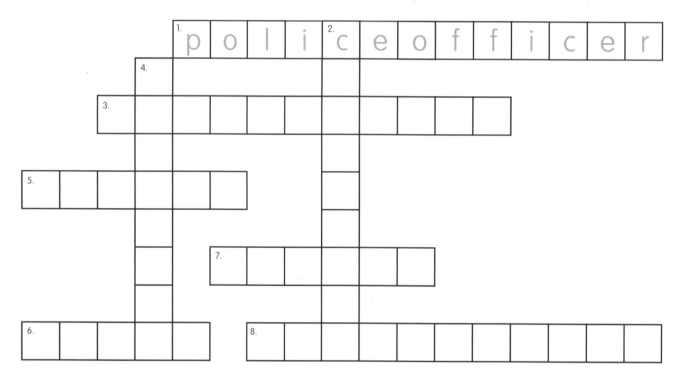

B. Write.

1.  I want to be a cook .

2. I want to be a _____.

3. I want to be a _____.

4. I want to be a _____.

Review

1. Animals

A. Write 3 words.

- _____ bird
- _____ dog
- _____ cat

B. Write the words in alphabetical order.

1. _____ bird
2. _____ cat
3. _____ dog

2. Body Parts

A. Write 3 words.

- _____
- _____
- _____

B. Write the words in alphabetical order.

1. _____
2. _____
3. _____

3. Colors, Patterns and Shapes

A. Write 3 words.

- _____
- _____
- _____

B. Write the words in alphabetical order.

1. _____
2. _____
3. _____

4. Clothing and Accessories

A. Write 3 words.

- _____
- _____
- _____

B. Write the words in alphabetical order.

1. _____
2. _____
3. _____

5. Food and Drink

A. Write 3 words.

- _____
- _____
- _____

B. Write the words in alphabetical order.

1. _____
2. _____
3. _____

6. Fruit and Vegetables

A. Write 3 words.

- _____
- _____
- _____

B. Write the words in alphabetical order.

1. _____
2. _____
3. _____

7. Household and Electronics

A. Write 3 words.

- _____
- _____
- _____

B. Write the words in alphabetical order.

1. _____
2. _____
3. _____

8. People

A. Write 3 words.

- _____
- _____
- _____

B. Write the words in alphabetical order.

1. _____
2. _____
3. _____

9. School

A. Write 3 words.	B. Write the words in alphabetical order.
• _____	1. _____
• _____	2. _____
• _____	3. _____

10. Town

A. Write 3 words.	B. Write the words in alphabetical order.
• _____	1. _____
• _____	2. _____
• _____	3. _____

11. Transportation

A. Write 3 words.	B. Write the words in alphabetical order.
• _____	1. _____
• _____	2. _____
• _____	3. _____

12. Weather

A. Write 3 words.	B. Write the words in alphabetical order.
• _____	1. _____
• _____	2. _____
• _____	3. _____

This certificate is presented to

_____

Student's name

for completing

Longman Children's
Picture Dictionary

Workbook 2

Congratulations!

_____   _____

Date   Teacher

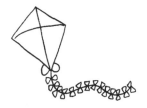